HOW DID THEY BUILD THAT?
ROAD

BY SHARON NITTINGER

COMMUNITY CONNECTIONS

CHERRY
LAKE
Publishing

Published in the United States of America by Cherry Lake Publishing
Ann Arbor, Michigan
www.cherrylakepublishing.com

Content Advisers: Nancy Kristof and Bob Nittinger, Consultant Technical Director
Reading Adviser: Cecilia Minden-Cupp, PhD, Literacy Consultant

Photo Credits: Cover and pages 1, 13, 17, 19 and 21, photos courtesy of Dynapac; page 5,
©egd, used under license from Shutterstock, Inc.; page 7, ©Henryk Sadura, used under license
from Shutterstock, Inc.; pages 9 and 11, photos courtesy of Liebherr Construction Equipment
Company; page 15, ©Cary Kalscheuer, used under license from Shutterstock, Inc.

LIBRARY OF CONGRESS CATALOGING-IN-PUBLICATION DATA
Nittinger, Sharon, 1966—
  How did they build that? Road / by Sharon Nittinger.
      p. cm.—(Community connections)
  Includes index.
  ISBN-13: 978-1-60279-482-5
  ISBN-10: 1-60279-482-0
  1. Roads—Design and construction—Juvenile literature. I. Title. II. Title: Road.
  TE149.N58 2009
  625.7—dc22   2008045249

Cherry Lake Publishing would like to acknowledge the
work of The Partnership for 21st Century Skills. Please
visit www.21stcenturyskills.org for more information.

ROAD

CONTENTS

HOW DID THEY BUILD THAT?

MOVING VEHICLES FORWARD

Roads help people go from one place to another. Cars and trucks travel best on smooth roads. Look at the road outside your house. Are there lines painted on the road? Is it smooth or bumpy? Did you ever wonder how the road was built?

Roads help people get to school and work every day.

A group of people create a plan for a new road. Then the survey crew gets to work. The survey crew helps decide where to build the road.

Workers have to make room for the new road. They sometimes remove trees and rocks. They use big machines to move them.

A surveyor uses a special tool to take measurements. The measurements help planners decide where to build a new road.

A **bulldozer** is one kind of big machine. It is a tractor with a wide blade in the front. The wide blade is used to move dirt and rocks.

An **excavator** is another big machine. It digs deep holes.

An excavator can be used to help clear the way for a new road.

Think about your community. Where do you think it would be good to have a new road? Would any rocks or trees need to be moved out of the way to build it?

MAKING THE PATH FLAT

The trees and rocks were removed from the path. Earth haulers have taken away the soil. Now other machines can fill in holes and smooth down steep hills. **Front loaders** and **graders** help make the ground level and even.

A front loader works to level the ground for a road.

Front loaders carry and push soil where it needs to go. Then a grader spreads the soil over the ground and makes it more level.

Sometimes new roads are needed when old ones wear out. The old road is torn up by a machine called a planer. Then the new road can be built.

A planer tears up an old road. Planers are also called milling machines.

CREATE!

Pile some dry rice on a cookie sheet. Use a plastic knife to push the rice. Pretend it is a grader pushing soil for a road. What happens to the rice after you push it with the knife?

A **concrete** mixer mixes stone, cement, and water to make concrete. Special machines turn the concrete into curbs and **gutters**. Curbs help keep cars and trucks on roads. Curbs and gutters let water flow off the road and into pipes under the road.

These concrete curbs are dry. Now workers can keep working on the road.

MAKE A GUESS!

When the concrete dries, more work is done on the road. What do you think the workers do while they wait for the concrete to harden?

MANY LAYERS

A roadway is made of many layers. Each layer must be smooth and strong.

Many roadways are made of **asphalt**. Asphalt is sticky and black. It is heated and mixed with sand and stone to make asphalt cement.

Can you see the black asphalt being loaded into this machine?

Dump trucks bring asphalt cement to the worksite. The dump trucks put the asphalt into a **paver**. A paver lays the asphalt on the road. This machine moves very slowly. Asphalt is hot and very sticky when it is placed on the road.

Some pavers are very big!

19

Rollers flatten all the layers of the road. The rollers smooth the asphalt. Now the roadway is completely paved. Lines are painted on the road. Lines help direct traffic and keep drivers safe.

The road is complete and ready for drivers to enjoy. Other roads are waiting to be built. Maybe one will be built near your house!

Rollers smooth out the asphalt. Soon this road will be ready for traffic.

GLOSSARY

asphalt (ASS-fawlt) a material used to make roads; it is made from oil and is blended with sand and stone

bulldozer (BUHL-doh-zuhr) a heavy machine with a blade in front for moving land

concrete (KON-kreet) strong building material made from cement, sand, gravel, and water

excavator (EKS-kuh-vay-tur) a machine that digs deep holes

front loaders (FRUHNT LOHD-urz) machines with a large bucket that carries and puts heavy items such as soil and rocks into trucks

graders (GRAYD-urz) machines used to move and spread soil

gutters (GUHT-urz) lower areas along the side of a road for rain water to drain off the road

paver (PAYV-ur) a machine that spreads a layer of asphalt or concrete on roads

FIND OUT MORE

BOOKS

Knudsen, Shannon, and Shannon Zemlicka. *From Rock to Road.* Minneapolis: Lerner Publications, 2004

Macken, JoAnn Early. *Building a Road.* Mankato, MN: Capstone Press, 2008

WEB SITES

Kikki's Workshop—We Love Construction Equipment
www.kenkenkikki.jp/e_index.html
Information, pictures, and games about all kinds of construction equipment

What Roads Are Made Of
www.chevroncars.com/learn/cars/roads
Read about the history of what roads have been made of

INDEX

ABOUT THE AUTHOR

Sharon Nittinger never gave much thought to roads until she met Bill, her husband. He and his father, Bob, have more than 35 years of combined experience working for Dynapac USA, a construction equipment manufacturer. Sharon has two children and turns to books to help answer the questions they ask her.